Little Pebble™

Staying Safe

Science Safety

by Sarah L. Schuette

Consultant: Shonette Doggett, coalition coordinator
Safe Kids Greater East Metro/St. Croix Valley
St. Paul, Minnesota

PEBBLE
a capstone imprint

Little Pebble is published by Pebble
1710 Roe Crest Drive
North Mankato, Minnesota 56003
www.mycapstone.com

Library of Congress Cataloging-in-Publication Data
Names: Schuette, Sarah L., 1976– author.
Title: Science safety / by Sarah L. Schuette.
Description: North Mankato, Minnesota : Pebble a Capstone imprint, [2020] | Series: Little pebble. Staying safe! | Audience: Ages 6–8. | Audience: K to grade 3. | Includes bibliographical references and index.
Identifiers: LCCN 2018058512| ISBN 9781977108692 (hardcover) | ISBN 9781977110329 (pbk.) | ISBN 9781977108777 (ebook pdf) Subjects: LCSH: Science—Experiments—Safety measures—Juvenile literature.
Classification: LCC Q182.3 .S2875 2020 | DDC 502.8/9—dc23
LC record available at https://lccn.loc.gov/2018058512

Editorial Credits
Erika L. Shores, editor; Heidi Thompson, designer; Morgan Walters, media researcher; Marcy Morin, scheduler; Tori Abraham, production specialist

Photo Credits
All photos by Capstone Studio/Karon Dubke

All internet sites appearing in back matter were available and accurate when this book was sent to press.

The author dedicates this book to her favorite scientist, Nicolas J. Pester, Geology and Chemistry Ph.D.

Printed and bound in China.
001671

Table of Contents

Time to Learn

Experiments help you learn.

But you need to be safe.

Always ask an adult to help.

What to Wear

Mac wears gloves.

They keep his hands clean.

Will wears a lab coat.

It covers his clothes.

Rosa wears safety glasses.

They keep her eyes safe.

What to Do

Mac never puts
anything in his mouth.

SCIENCE SAFETY

Follow the Teacher's Rules.

Do Not Put Things in Your Mouth.

Wash Your Hands.

Be Careful with Tools.

Use Goggles and Proper Clothing.

Think Responsibly.

13

Be careful!

Rosa lets an adult pour.

Stand back!

Rosa watches

from a safe place.

Clean up!

Will wipes up spills.

He washes his hands.

Learning Fun

Follow the rules.

Stay safe.

Science is fun.

Glossary

experiment—a scientific test in which you perform a series of actions and carefully observe their effects in order to learn about something

gloves—a covering for your hands; gloves can be plastic or rubber

lab coat—a coat or apron to protect your clothing and body from spills

Read More

Berne, Emma Carlson. *Predict!: Plan an Experiment.* The Scientific Method in Action. New York: PowerKids Press, 2015.

Rowe, Brooke. *Building a Volcano.* My Science Fun. Ann Arbor, MI: Cherry Lake Publishing, 2017.

Shores, Lori. *How to Build a Fizzy Rocket.* Hands-on Science Fun. North Mankato, MN: Capstone, 2018.

Internet Sites

Kids Science Experiments
www.lovemyscience.com/lab-rules.html

Science Experiments for Kids
www.sciencekids.co.nz/experiments.html

Super-cool stuff!

Check out projects, games, and lots more at
www.capstonekids.com

Critical Thinking Questions

1. What should you wear in a science lab?

2. Where should you watch an experiment?

3. What should you do when you are done with an experiment?

Index